SUMMER: NO LOVE: THE REAL
SHAKE: YOUNG LOVE: STRANGER:
BREAKING THROUGH: NOW:
SUDDENLY LAVENDER: THE CLUB:
THRILLS: WALK ON THE SAND:
THE STOVE: HIDING: WOMIN:
LEMONS: CHI CHI: AGE: ARCH: YOU:
GRANT ME YOUR LOVE: TALENT:
ANNIVERSARY: RED CAP: HELLO
TITTY: HEAD LIGHTS: BREATHING:
LOCKING: IRIDESCENCE

HELLO TITTY

MARTHA ACKROYD CURTIS

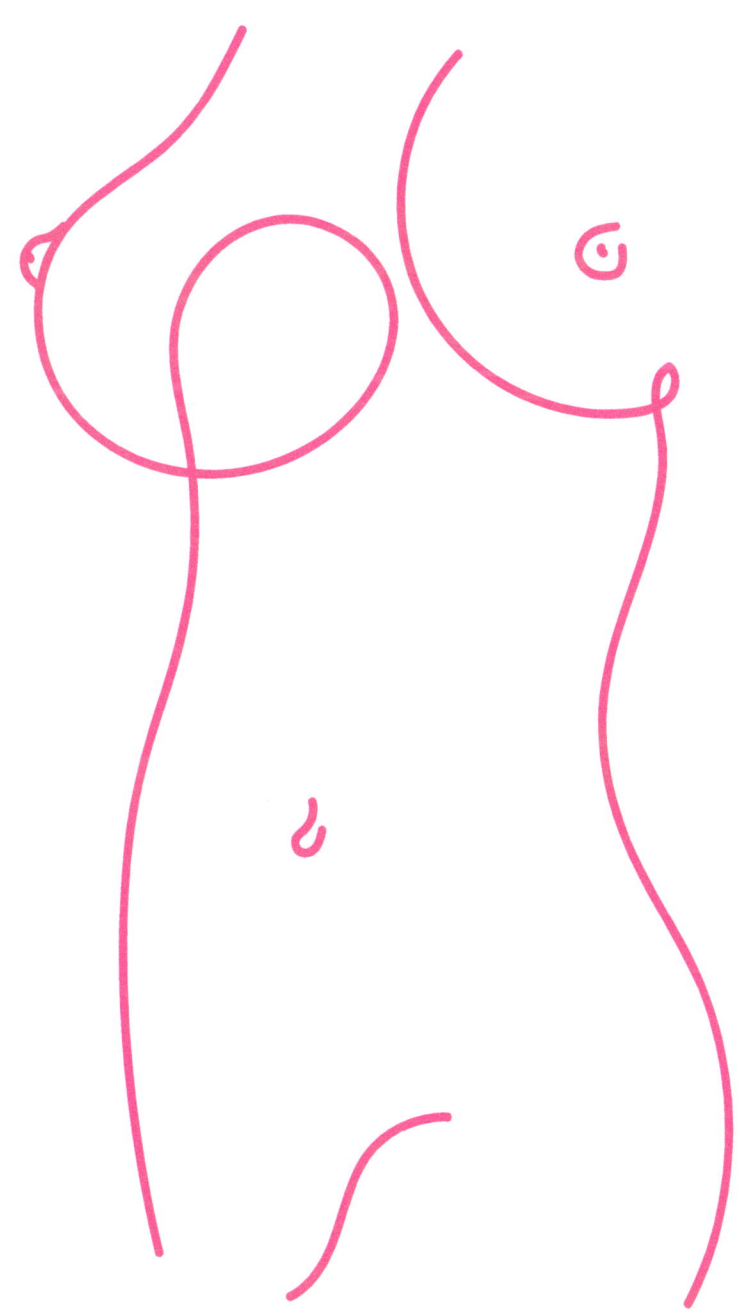

First published by Busybird Publishing 2020

Copyright © 2020 Martha Ackroyd Curtis

ISBN
978-1-922465-04-7 (softcover)
978-1-922465-11-5 (hardcover)

This book is copyright. Apart from any fair dealing for the purposes of study, research, criticism, review, or as otherwise permitted under the Copyright Act, no part may be reproduced by any process without written permission. Enquiries should be made through the publisher.

This is a work of fiction. Any similarities between places and characters are a coincidence.

Cover image: Kev Howlett

Layout Design / typesetting: Kev Howlett - Busybird Publishing

Busybird Publishing
2/118 Para Road
Montmorency, Victoria
Australia 3094
www.busybird.com.au

ABOUT:

Martha Ackroyd Curtis is an Australian video, installation and multi- medium artist. Her work consists of large-scale installation art, which is formulated through cohesive conceptual design. She has exhibited extensively in Australia and overseas, and participated in various art festivals. Although known publicly as a visual artist, she has always written. In her art practice there has always been a poetic license. Her art journals are in a sense now being opened up and released. The photographs chosen for this volume are selected based on delicacy, a little bit of smut, power, and an extra strong dosage of humour. This is her first published volume. ENJOY.

FOR ALL WOMEN KIND

SUMMER

It was a Melbourne summer
An accent spoke to me
Some how we ended up, front of the stage
A queer memento
I danced with her, thighs between mine
Oblivious to the scene we made
We had no cares at all
That girl and I

NO LOVE

When it is your first
When it is unrequited
You never forget
Even when you had those moments
Moments with no ending
No love back, only feeling inside you
The yearning
And hurting
The vacuum suction of your body
Disposing it
But you never forget
The first one

THE REAL SHAKE

I remember grabbing with lust
Thrusting her bust
Shaking so much
Knowing this is real, this is real
From lust to love
Aah Love the magic ingredient
And yes you prove it
And aah yes and she knows it

YOUNG LOVE

We sitting on sand
Young skin, a tan
Talking about our plans
Our future
Laughing, holding hands

We are old now
Hair is grey
I stopped dying it
I am still holding her hand
We still have plans
We have nieces and nephews
We rock back on our chairs
We are laughing and happy
She still is just the same
She still laughs at the moments and cries at the times
We are young and older
With fake hips and maybe creaky knees
But we can still dance from the night into the dawn

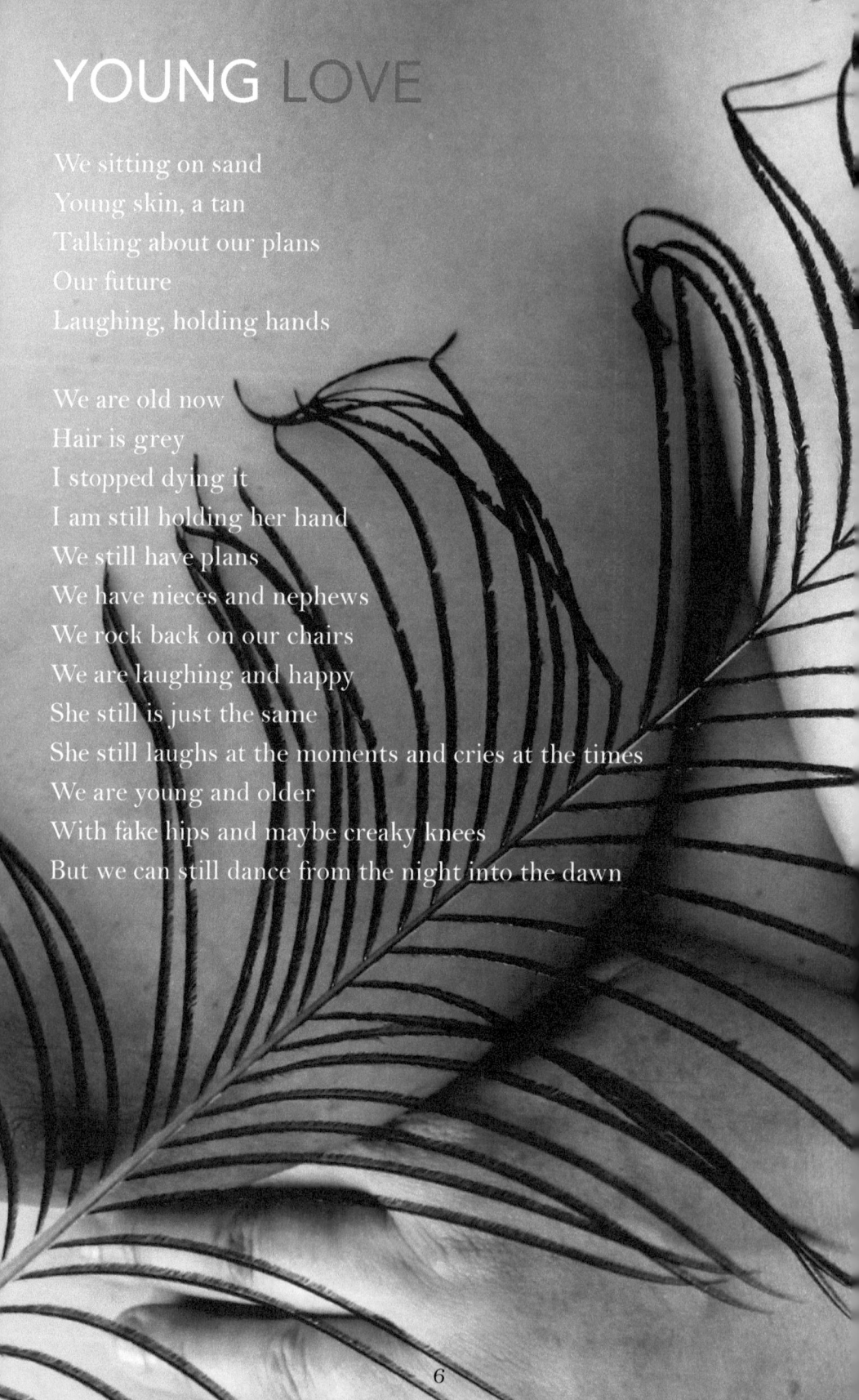

STRANGER

I look beneath her hair
Covering bounty
I am nervous
Meeting this beautiful stranger from the place
The dance floor
From the beats a rhythm begins
We punctuate each other movements
Throbbing together
Like a disco
PRIDE
beat
Pumping, grinding, and then

BREAKING THROUGH

The old couple sitting
Wrinkles over bodies
Cuddling by the stoves flames
That,
Are warming their kind home
They once were thought
Of
As a myth
That there kind
Just did not exist
How they hid
Kissed only amongst the allied
Then they awoke chests out yelling
We are here!
And loving, out of the shadows

NOW

They watch the young ones
Old couple
Are proud
That they can see that
Freedom
That visibility
That humanity.
And they kiss now on their verandah
And walk at pride
Smiling down that boulevard
Because they were never, ever
A myth.

SUDDENLY LAVENDER

Suddenly
Lavender stole a gaze
My horse harness
Raised
Like arched backs onto buttocks
As I lay writing a rhythm
On her rump
A poets folly
A sweet hearts
Hum

THE CLUB

The place is no more
This is a documentary
I am that post on insta'
Years ago
Where hips grind and common thought combined
Was on that dancing floor
OXOX
LED, LED, LED

THRILLS

Thrills and spills
Cosmic drills
A looking glass caste dark
Over the Fallen few
She rises against the night of dark
Her hips
Wetter

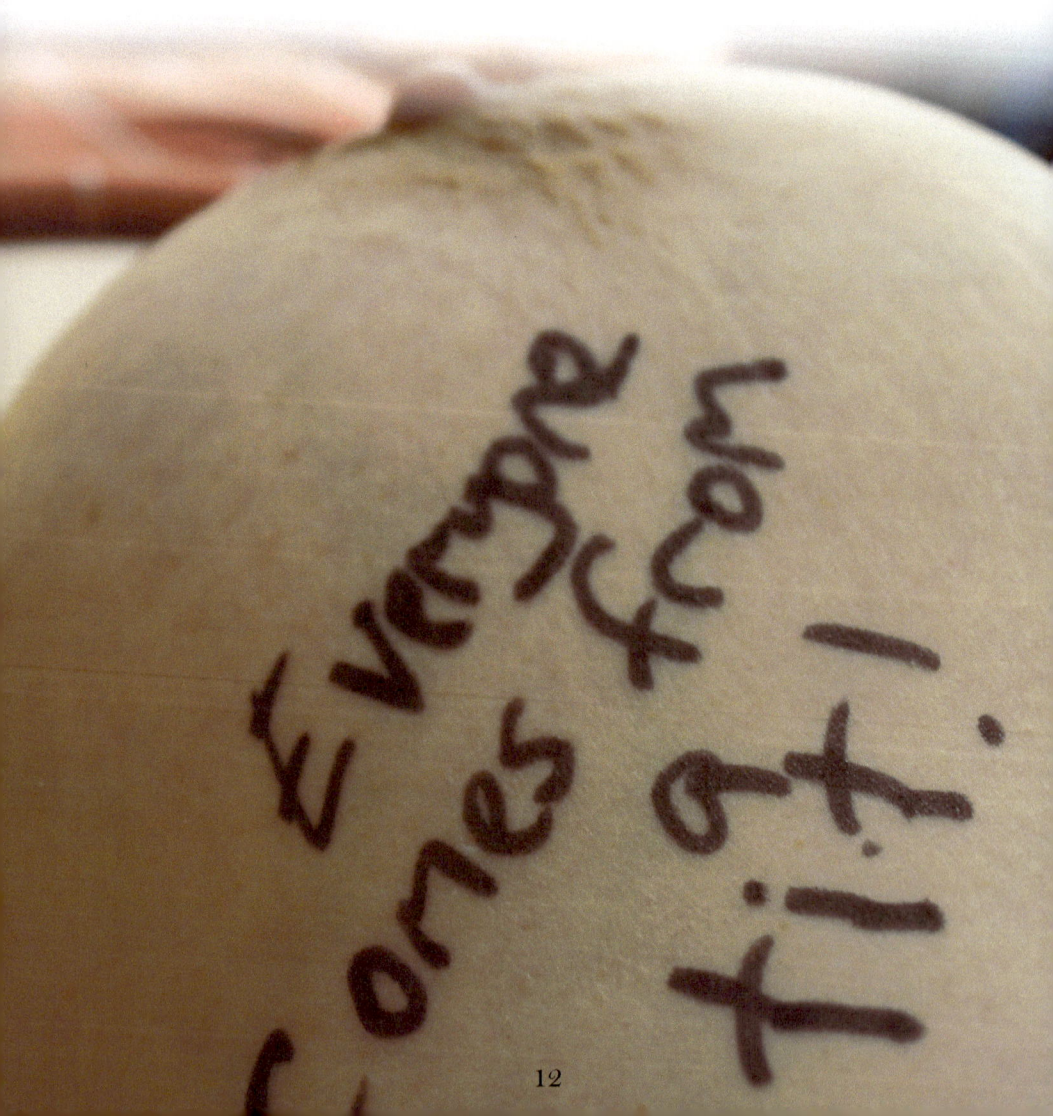

WALK ON THE SAND

Massage between toes
Soulfully frolic
We mermaids
Of seaweed hair
We shriek at ships
If a woman overboard
We coax her to the living
But
If lungs full
We hold her till last breath
And weep
Boat holes
Of sailors going down
To meet John Dory

THE STOVE

I sit on the grey couch
I smell the delights of her offering
KD Lang filling ears
A greeting of sublimity
She maybe crotchety
In the kitchen
Perfection
Cuisine queen
But the delicacy and patience
Of creation is
A lovemaking

HIDING

She shy
Face blushing tomatoes
I brush the hair off
Laughing
Sunlight dancing on faces
When we first kissed
My big nose would meet her eyes
I kiss her a lot all over
As the sun dances
Over hills

WOMIN

Womin I need ya
Womin I curl my toes
Womin I need ya when my tobacco unfurls
My cigarette I light
Place between lip
Leg in thigh
In the haze of night
Head on belly
I seek your bosom
Weary head
Hear your chest
I know life's importance
Resting with you

LEMONS

We walk round the corner
Suburban acceptance
Holding hands
Abundant of fruits
A lemon tree
Overhang footpath
Legs up and grab
Laugh
A lemon
Strong hands

CHI CHI

Our little one lies there
Princess
POPPY, POPPY, POPPY
Seeded life
A character of paws and furs
Leap
Our baby
Softly
Beating chest

AGE

When age spots fill our hands
And our bodies have folds of time and journey
I know

I know that if I have stick or you have motorized
granny buggy
We will have each other
If you leave early or I leave late
Or I leave early and you leave late

ARCH

Come with me crumbling arch
admit it you wave to me
golden tressils curtain me
your not clinically but capable

Where are the years going
Where have the days gone
I'm aging fast
There is no stopping it
But I will step out of the door
Always with you

YOU

The irreplaceable you, whispers in my ear…
All the good things of this world,
And all the ladders at all the curly curls that grow between your limbs, like shiny black arches on your skin…

GRANT ME YOUR LOVE

Hold out your hand and I will stroke it
I will love you till your blind and wrinkly and cannot
Pee into toilet
I will love you till a walk for you is to the back door
I will love you if you are bald and balmy
I will love you and meet you at the golden gates…

TALENT

She could NOT do 'anything's', at school sport, maths, science
One day the circus came to school
She found herself juggling each day after school
She found her thang…
At 20 she had joined the circus and was riding the horses and flipping on the trapeze
There goes 'I can't do anythings'.

VA

PARIS

MAY
£3.90

**INC-COUTURE
WHAT SHE REALLY
WEARS**

ANNIVERSARY

Anniversary bring me closer
To the state of now
Throw my arms around her
Don't waste time
You need to remember this
It needs to be a good one
Inside
Girl I love you
Sometimes it hurts
The times I yell
I don't mean
My passion is for you
You are my fruit
In the wood bowl
And I share the nectarine with you

RED CAP

I wanted the little red cap
I was 4 years old
Not understanding my mothers confusion
Why does she want this cap?
My mother did not like caps
I liked it
Boys wore them
UNFAIR IF I COULD NOT
I was able to wear my fathers old
Red school cricket cap
I would hide under it shyly
When we walked to Prahran market

The new red cap
My mother gave into it
I wore it proudly
I obtained a sense of confidence
Pride I think it is called
I was only 4
I felt that power upon my head

Today I understand the background
The social anxiety of the parent
At the time

These
TIMES
I do hope things have changed
We at any age can wear
What the heart says

HELLO TITTY

I remember them growing
Out of chest
Sore

I did not realize their magic
Until a lovers warm touch
Her hands like velvet on the skin
Hers like rose buds in the spring

In the symphony of beating chest
Ours lovers love heaving at each breast
Knowing more of their magic
As we share
Each which
Only we can bare

HEAD LIGHTS

TITS ON HIGH BEAM
We drive home
The taxi feels like sex
Want to open her pants in there
We reach
Bedroom
Passion
Passion
Passion
Next morning
I get no
Number
Maybe
Sex
Was
It
I
Wait
For
HER.

BREATHING

BREATHING ON SKIN
GOOSEBUMPS
BACK BONES
HOT COLD SWEAT
TONGUE
CHEEK
EYES
CHEST
LEGS
HAIR
INSIDE
BETWEEN
HOT
HEAT
HEAVY
BREATHE
RELEASE

SUCK
KNOWING
SEEING
CLOSING
EYES
MEETING
TOGETHER
TOTAL
IMPACT
OF
DESIRE

LOCKING

Crossing the street
Happy and gay
Looking out through shades
Another sees you
Black ray bans
Long brown hair
She stared
You want to wink
But you are both
Wearing shades
Can you be sure
Sure
The world really
Does
Not
Just
Revolve
Around
You
LOCK EYES

IRIDESCENCE

IREDESCENCE HAZE
Meeting eyes
Glazed over
Doughnuts

The frenetic frequency of unknown solitude
Plays the frets
On her
She moves
The tune is
When a heart beat
SKIPS
TURNING HEADS
BODY
ARCHES
Light distorts
In
Crystal
The
Disk

Of my
Dreams
SUCCUMBS
In the abscess
Where pus and mellow
Dissolve
And
Truth
Takes
Hold
As
She
Clasps
My
Strong
Hand

My saliva is like hot metal on ground
Silver
Is the solitary pleasure

ORGASM SHAKES FUCKING GROUND

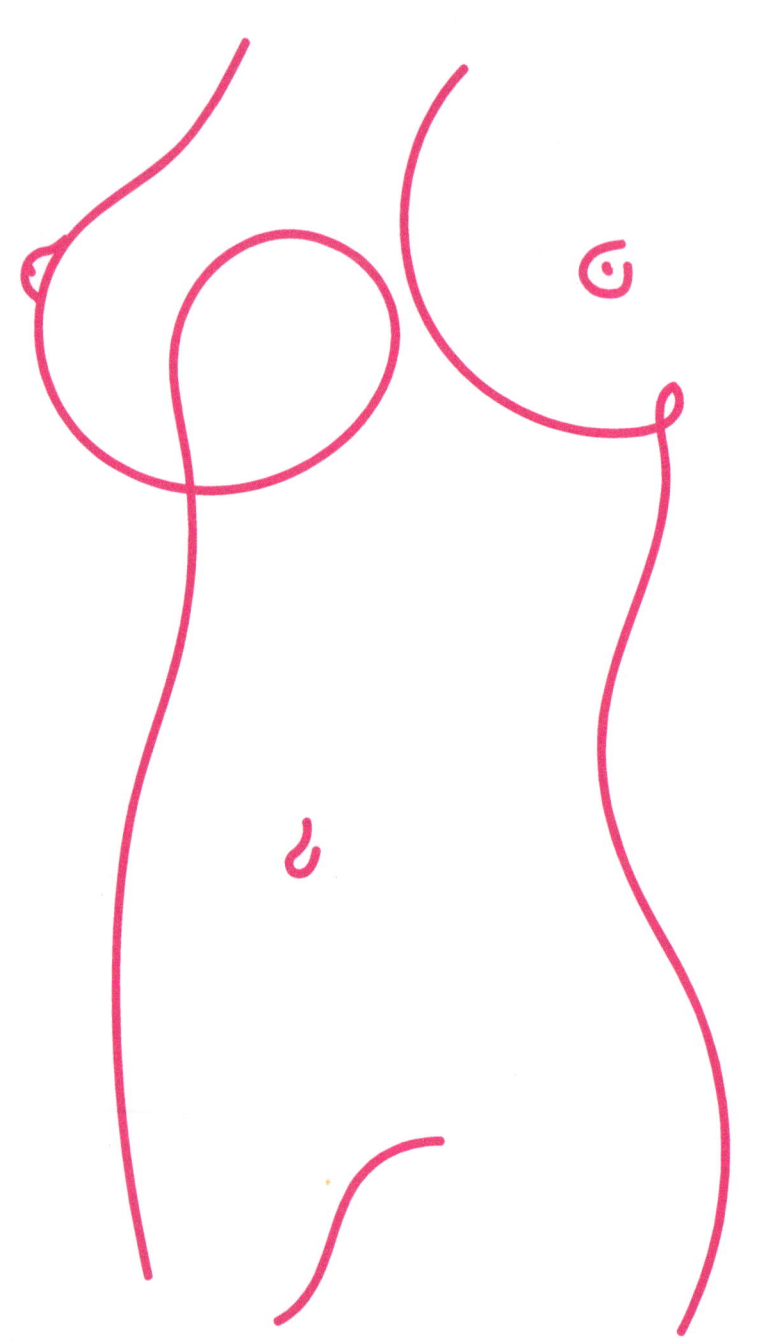

www.ingramcontent.com/pod-product-compliance
Lightning Source LLC
LaVergne TN
LVHW070918080526
838202LV00017B/2256